DATE DUE

COUNSEL FROM
AN ALLY

COUNSEL FROM AN ALLY

*Reflections on Changes
within the
Atlantic Community*

ANDRÉ PHILIP

The John Findley Green Foundation Lectures
1965

University of Missouri Press • *Columbia*

Green Foundation Lectures

THE John Findley Green Foundation was established by the late Mrs. Green in 1937 as a memorial of her husband, who was a graduate of Westminster College in the Class of 1884 and served as a member of the college's Board of Trustees for twenty-seven years.

The Deed of Gift provides for lectures designed to promote understanding of economic, political, and social problems of international concern.

Mr. Green's lifelong belief that the most practical application of the Christian religion is the improvement of human relations makes this Foundation an especially fitting memorial of his life and work.

Lectures on the Green Memorial Foundation

Oscar D. Skelton, *then Undersecretary for Foreign Affairs for the Dominion of Canada.* SOME GAINS AND LOSSES OF THE PRESENT GENERATION. *University of Chicago Press, 1937.*

John Langdon-Davies. CONFLICT BETWEEN DEMOCRACY AND FASCISM IN EUROPE. *Unpublished. 1938.*

Francis B. Sayre, *former High Commissioner to the Philippines.* THE PROTECTION OF AMERICAN EXPORT TRADE. *University of Chicago Press, 1939.*

T. V. Smith, *Member of Congress and Professor of Philosophy at the University of Chicago.* THE LEGISLATIVE WAY OF LIFE. *University of Chicago Press, 1940.*

Carlo Sforza, *former Ambassador for Italy to China, to*

Turkey, and to France and subsequently Italian Minister for Foreign Affairs. THE TOTALITARIAN WAR AND AFTER. *University of Chicago Press, 1941; George Allen & Unwin, Ltd., 1942.*

Samuel Guy Inman, *Lecturer on Latin-American Relations at the University of Pennsylvania and Yale University.* PAN-AMERICAN POSTWAR PROGRAM. *Unpublished. 1942.*

Winston Churchill, *former Prime Minister of England, who was introduced by* President Harry S Truman. THE SINEWS OF PEACE. *Lecture broadcast over worldwide radio chains. Westminster College, 1946.*

Reinhold Niebuhr, *Professor of Applied Christian Ethics, Union Theological Seminary.* THIS NATION UNDER GOD. *In* THE IRONY OF AMERICAN HISTORY. *Charles Scribner's Sons, 1952.*

J. C. Penney, *merchant.* THE SPIRITUAL BASIS FOR IMPROVING HUMAN RELATIONS. *Privately published. 1949.*

Roscoe Pound, *Dean Emeritus of Harvard Law School.* JUSTICE ACCORDING TO LAW. *Yale University Press, 1951.*

Charles H. Malik, *Ambassador for Lebanon.* THE CRISIS OF REASON. *Unpublished. 1953.*

Harry S Truman, *former President of the United States.* WHAT HYSTERIA DOES TO US *and* PRESIDENTIAL PA-

PERS, THEIR IMPORTANCE AS HISTORICAL DOCUMENTS. *The first of these lectures and other public addresses and papers of the President, edited by Professor David Horton, are in* FREEDOM AND EQUALITY. *University of Missouri Press, 1960.*

Guy E. Snavely, *former Executive Secretary of the Association of American Colleges.* COLLEGE AND CHURCH IN AMERICA. *In* THE CHURCH AND THE FOUR-YEAR COLLEGE. *Harper and Brothers, 1955.*

Stanley N. Barnes, *Judge, Ninth Circuit of the United States Court of Appeals.* GOVERNMENT AND BIG BUSINESS. *Unpublished. 1956.*

William Yandell Elliott, *Williams Professor of Government at Harvard University.* THE USES AND LIMITS OF THE UNITED NATIONS IN RELATION TO AMERICAN FOREIGN POLICY *and* MEETING THE POLITICAL STRATEGY AND TACTICS OF THE SOVIET AND CHINESE COMMUNIST BLOC IN THE POST-STALIN PERIOD. *Published in part in* THE IDEA OF COLONIALISM, *Strausz-Hupe and Hazard, eds. Praeger, for the Foreign Policy Research Institute of the University of Pennsylvania, 1957.*

Edward McCrady, *Vice Chancellor and President of the University of the South.* FREEDOM AND CAUSALITY. *Unpublished. 1958.*

The Rt. Hon. the Viscount Hailsham, Q.C., *Lord Privy*

Contents

xi

I

THE NEW FRANCE

IN these three lectures I shall attempt to describe the problems we are facing in Europe at the present time. In my first lecture I am going to speak chiefly of my country, France, and of the tremendous changes presently taking place, both in our technical life and in our economic, social, and political institutions. In my second lecture I shall speak of the unification of Europe and of the pressing problems we face in the economic and trade relations between Europe and other industrialized countries. This is a central issue in the so-called "Kennedy round" of tariff negotiations; this was a problem of last year's Geneva Conference on World Trade Development. In my last lecture I shall consider the general problems of French and European foreign policy and conclude by presenting some proposals on how we could build a new Atlantic Alliance on a constructive and more nearly equal basis.

First, what is happening in France at the present time? As I told you, a tremendous change began immediately after the Second World War and the liberation of our territory. I say "a tremendous change" because in the whole of the nineteenth century France had lagged behind Germany, the United States, and Great Britain in its economic evolution. We missed the first agricultural revolution, which was realized by Great Britain at the end of the eighteenth century. We missed it because the French Revolution created the French pattern of landholding, characterized by very small, individually owned portions. We missed the second agricultural revolution, at the end of the nineteenth century, when Holland and Denmark changed from wheat-producing countries to meat-producing countries. France, at this time, remained chiefly a wheat- and wine-producing country, producing for internal consumption and protected by a high tariff. At the same time, in the nineteenth century, we began to industrialize, but we did so very slowly, through family firms that advanced by reinvesting their profits. These family enterprises were reluctant to borrow from the banking system, to go to the financial market, and to create big companies. Lacking capital and savings and influenced by the financial advice of the French private banks, French capitalists hesitated to invest their savings in French industries. Rather, they preferred to purchase the bonds of foreign governments; these were called Family Fathers Undertaking. So, they invested in the bonds of the Russian Government and lost absolutely everything. Finally, the nation's state of mind in the nineteenth century lacked a spirit of risk-taking. This expressed itself in the declining birth rate. France was becoming an old country, led by old people.

Many of these old attitudes have changed since the liberation, as a result of a fact and two choices. The fact is the same as the one you have known here in America and which you have called the "baby boom." The birth rate in France rose rather quickly immediately after the liberation, partly as a result of a law passed in 1940, three days before the fall of France. This law, the last legislation enacted by the Third French Republic, introduced the family allowances system. It is now no longer a tragedy to have children, and it may even sometimes become a pleasant undertaking. Our population has increased to nearly fifty million inhabitants. We have a younger generation coming of age, entering into the productive process, asking that its voice be heard and that it be allowed to take part in all important decisions.

The big change is that now the new generation is taking an active part in French economic, social, and political life. This means a complete change in the whole national attitude toward the world's different problems. This is the fact.

We also made two choices, both of them at the time of the Fourth Republic. The first was the choice in favor of European unification, of which I will speak in this lecture. The second was the choice in favor of the French system of flexible economic planning. Our First Plan, inaugurated by Jean Monnet as Director of the Planning Department, aimed at rebuilding everything that had been destroyed during the war. It succeeded. Then, the Second Plan tried to direct investment in all of the basic industries, and it succeeded. The Third Plan aimed at rationalizing the whole of French economic life. We are now in the process of preparing the Fifth Plan, which will be put in operation from 1966 to 1971.

Now, first of all, how are these plans drawn up? We have a national planning department — a very small administration of no more than a hundred men, but first-class men all of them — which closely follows the nation's economic life, prepares estimates and predictions on economic matters somewhat akin to the economic report to the President here in the United States, and tries to estimate the rate and direction of economic evolution in the next five years and to state what choices will have to be made. For the Fifth Plan these experts prepared three projections — one for an increase of the national product of 4 per cent, one of 5 per cent, and one of 6 per cent. They calculated in the three cases what would be the necessary investments, the volume of imports and exports, the expenses for research, the level of collective and private consumption. Their projections were debated in the French Parliament just two months ago; after a very important debate, the Parliament accepted, as a basis for planning, the projection of a 5 per cent increase in the gross national product and a 4 per cent increase in the national consumption.

Now that Parliament has made this decision, the plan goes to what we call "modernization committees," both for sectors of the economy and for the economic regions of the country. The sectoral modernization committees are organized industry by industry — automobiles, chemicals, steel, etc. These committees are composed of representatives of employers and of trade unions in each industry. France is divided into twenty-two regions. The regional modernization committees are elected by the people and are made up of employers, workmen, farmers, representatives of the universities, and representatives from local elected bodies. All of these committees prepare reports; the reports go to the national planning department, which then draws up the final plan. The plan then is discussed, on a technical level, by the National Economic and Social Council — a body composed of workers and employers — and then is sent to the Parliament for final ratification.

What happens after a plan has been adopted for realization? We have in the French economy two sectors, the public sector and the private sector. For the public sector, which means for the national administration and for the nationalized industries, the plan is compulsory. More and more the national budget has become the final financial translation of the economic plan. In the private sector, the plan is only incitative. Private enterprises do what they want, provided they realize the aim established for them in the plan. The instruments and the ways and means of achieving these levels may be chosen by the private businessmen, but attractive inducements are offered those who realize the plan, such as obtaining tax reductions, subventions; chiefly, if they fully realize the plan, they receive the Legion of Honor, which is a very important incentive!

This, essentially, is the way French economic planning works. The very curious thing is that after much discussion and violent disputes, there is now a unanimous consensus in France on the actual practice of flexible planning. There is, of course, a lot of discussion. Some people say the plan relies too much on incentives and should be more compulsory; others say it is too compulsory and should offer more incentives; still others say it ought to cover the whole policy of incomes; and others say it is very difficult to devise a general income policy. A great deal of discussion is going on, but the value of flexible planning of the nation's economy is now accepted by nearly everyone — workers, farmers, and most of all, of course, university economists.

The result, in part, of the plan has been many technical and social changes in our country. The first one is an agricultural revolution, at last. In the past five years, agricultural production has increased by 9 per cent per year, and agricultural productivity per acre has risen 4.5 per cent per year, which is a rate of growth a little higher than the average progress in industry. For the first time in our history, agriculture is progressing at a higher rate than industry. The first change is that there are now too many farmers — you know the same thing in America — and that a great many of our young farmers are leaving the land and seeking work in industry. The farmers remaining on the land differ sharply from their fathers. The old French peasant was a man whose aim in life was to buy land. He devoted all the money he had to buying land, so that after acquiring ownership of land he had no capital left to work it. He never went into debt; borrowing from a bank meant for him a loss of personal independence. In his mind, borrowing was the beginning of bankruptcy. The young farmers today are entirely different. They do not yearn to buy land; they have no passion to own land. Rather, they prefer to rent both house and land, provided the rent is not too high, and to use all their own money and the money they can borrow from the bank — because they do borrow heavily, too heavily sometimes — to buy cattle, machinery, and scientific implements. They are becoming agricultural businessmen, entirely different from the old type of peasant that we have had in France.

This new generation of young farmers, with their new attitudes, is bringing about changes in the countryside and stirring up some conflicts. First, they want to have land rights. Recently a law called the Farm Law was enacted. It provided that in every regional unit a farmers cooperative, with help from the national administration, would get a pre-emption right on any land offered for sale. The farmer now has the legal right to buy this land. No one else may buy if the farmer says, "I am buying it." The price is fixed by a court, and no outsider can say, "I will offer a higher price, and I want to buy." Thus, pre-emption rights for farmers are at a price fixed by the court. Either the purchaser sells the land to young farmers or rents it to them while keeping the ownership. This practice is increasing.

The second change is the gradual disappearance of the middleman. Until recently, French agriculture was dominated by the middleman, who bought produce from the farmers and sold it in the cities. Now, many of these middlemen are being squeezed out of business by a double pressure, coming from the farmers' organized cooperatives on the one hand and, on the other hand, from commercial business in the cities, organized into new modern capitalist trade organizations, like the supermarket. After having eliminated the middleman, the farmers cooperatives and the supermarkets, for a time, faced each other and fought, one against the other. Now, they are beginning to work out cooperative arrangements. In Paris some months ago, the first supermarket was organized by a mixed company composed of modern tradesmen and farmers cooperatives who got together to create this new enterprise.

Then, too, increasing speculation in real estate has created a threat to farmers. New highways have made the countryside more accessible to city dwellers, so more people are buying houses in the country. Beginning in the South of France, but now becoming generalized everywhere, speculation in real estate has quickened, and the farmers are protesting. In the West of France — the most conservative part of our country in the past — the farmers associations are asking now for socialization of the land by which the town council or the regional organization may become the owner of the land, rent it either to farmers cooperatives or to people building houses, and thus curb the real estate speculators, against whom there is a unanimity of protest in the country. It is apparent from these statements that a tremendous change is going on in the French agriculture. It is under the leadership of a new organization called the Young Farmers' Association, which is taking the lead among cooperative organizations in modernizing methods of production.

In French industry we find at the moment two very different kinds of change. On the one hand, the working class of unskilled and semiskilled workers is slowly and progressively decreasing in number, just as in America, and I believe that in fifty years this working class will have entirely disappeared. But, during the transitional period, a very acute human problem has been created. There is a melancholy future for this old working class because they have lost all the hopes they ever had. They were the backbone of the revolutionary spirit in France; now they see that there is no longer any real prospect of a revolution. They were the backbone of the Communist

movement; now they realize that in Russia the structure
of industry is not very different from what it is in America
or in France. This old working class is not satisfied with
the structure of industry as it is today because industry
is becoming more and more centralized and they have
to obey orders coming from above. You know that
Frenchmen hate most of all taking orders from above. A
recent inquiry shows that 80 per cent of the French semiskilled and unskilled workers, which are the backbone
of the Communist vote, now dream of becoming shop-
keepers, of leaving the industrial system to become again
independent producers. A trade union movement of
these workers and a political party based on their votes
progressively become the most conservative because
they oppose the new industrial technical revolution.
They are defending the marginal enterprises. Many people in this class are outside of what is happening in
France at the present time. This causes the greatest concern in our social and psychological life. The only way to
solve it is through the development of rapid technical
and professional education, so that, as soon as possible,
at least the young element of this unskilled working class
may become technicians — the unskilled may become
semiskilled, and sometime, perhaps, the semiskilled may
become skilled. But to advance from a skilled workman
to a technician one needs four years of study. This is a

barrier that at the present time is separating the old working class from the new one.

I come now to a new factor in French industrial life. It is what we call the new working class, or the salaried class, which includes everyone in what we call the *cadres*. There is no English word corresponding to our French word *cadres*. It includes everyone from the draftsman, the technical engineer, the foreman, and the majority of the white-collar workers to the general manager of the plant, and there is no exclusive separation. Within the *cadres*, one moves from one position to another. There is inner promotion. The same phenomenon exists in the United States, but in France these people are entirely unionized, more unionized than the unskilled workers. Since they are the people who are technically progressive, they ask to have their voices heard in the management of the enterprises. This is something quite new, quite different from what you are experiencing in the United States. In France we have a Works Committee in every industrial plant, introduced by the law. Elected by the workmen in every plant that employs more than fifty workmen, the Works Committee is active in social activities in the plant and is informed on all the technical and economic problems of management. The curious thing is that in the Works Committee the unskilled workers are interested only in social work;

they organize Christmas celebrations, libraries, cooperative restaurants and canteens, and vacation tours, and they take care of the sick. They are not, however, interested at all in the decisions taken in the plant. On the contrary, the representatives of the salaried class of the technicians always ask for information on everything going on in the plant and insist on taking part in the decisions of management.

Sometimes this interest on the part of the *cadres* in the operations of a local plant generates serious conflicts. An interesting dispute took place last year in the city of Grenoble, the strike of the Neypric plant. This firm builds dams and harbors all over the world. The plant in Grenoble is an experimental plant in which three-quarters of the expenses go for scientific research, carried on in cooperation with the Faculty of Sciences of the University of Grenoble. Now, far away in Paris, there was a merger among different financial groups. The new dominating group wanted to reduce expenditure on scientific research in the Neypric plant in Grenoble. The technicians at the plant called a strike; the workmen followed. The university supported the strike because it shared in the scientific research, and the City of Grenoble backed the strikers because the Neypric plant was one of the elements of the regional economic development of the whole of the Alpine region. There were tremendous street demonstrations. The police protected, rather than dispersed, a march in the streets of Grenoble. All the civic leaders of the city and the president of the university led this demonstration on behalf of the mutual interests of city, university, and technicians and of the regional economy against the financial domination of the Parisian bankers.* This whole affair expressed one of the changes taking place at the present time in France. This new social group that is taking the initiative is economically and technically progressive. It expresses itself in defending the regional economic development against the old centralized administration of Paris, which has endured since the time of the Kings of France, and which is now breaking up.

Curiously enough, this transformation, coming from the bottom of the economic life and from the new salaried class, is supported by a number of employers. We have a group that calls itself the Young Employers' Association, made up of businessmen less than forty years of age; when members pass their fortieth year, they are ousted. This Young Employers' Association, along with the salaried people, represents a new social force.

All of these economic and social changes have created a crisis in our political life that affects both traditional

---

* In the local elections in the spring of 1965, these civic leaders won a majority in the town council, and one of them is now mayor of Grenoble.

parliamentary institutions and the old political parties. One of Parliament's primary functions has entirely changed. Since the Six reached agreement last December in Brussels on a common agricultural policy for the Common Market, neither the French Parliament, nor the German, nor the Italian can any longer discuss agricultural matters. Laws concerning agriculture in the European Economic Community of Benelux, France, Italy, and West Germany are presently made at Brussels by the Commission of the European Economic Community. Very soon it will be the same for financial legislation, for the uses of energy, and for the automobile industry. A European parliament is urgently needed to control these decisions, since national parliaments no longer control decisions affecting these questions.

A second change is this: For many years the French Parliament functioned as a sounding board between the Government and the people. The Government explained its policy to the Parliament, then members of Parliament, every weekend, went to their constituencies to explain the Government's policy. The voters protested, as French people always do protest, and then the members of Parliament returned to Paris on Monday to lay the protests before the members of the Government and the heads of the administration. Now, that political process is finished. Today, when the French Government wants to explain something to the voters, a spokesman appears on television, and the people hear directly the Government's explanation; when the Government wants to know what the French people think, it takes a poll of public opinion. The present Government really governs with the instruments of the Gallup Poll, supplemented by the referendum. When the Government sees that, on a given point, its policy is supported by a majority of the people, it calls a referendum on this question. The Government always wins, since it calls a referendum only when the Gallup Poll shows that it has a majority. The Government never called a referendum on the French nuclear force, because the Gallup Poll showed that 75 per cent of the people opposed the *force de frappe*.

One of the imperative changes that will have to be introduced into our constitution, while keeping the referendum, is to allow the Parliament, too, the initiative of calling a referendum and not leave this decision in the hands of the President of the Republic. It is the reason for the change that is important. The power to call a referendum, which has been taken away under the present constitution, is the last shred of the legislative initiative possessed by the French Parliament. You find this loss of initiative by legislatures everywhere in Europe, even in Great Britain. It is quite clear that, in formulating an economic and financial plan for the next five years, the proportion of all expenditures for the next five years is thereby established, and, as a result, independent pieces of legislation that would destroy the balance of expenses and cause inflation can no longer be considered by the national legislature. Practically, the legislative power of the Assembly is progressively disappearing, and nobody can prevent this from happening. It appears that the function of the Assembly becomes essentially to vote the plan and to control the realization of the plan by different instruments. The first instrument is the question period. There, if the Government's response to the deputies' questions is not satisfactory, the Parliament can debate and can close the debate by passing a resolution indicating the policy it should like the Government to follow. Then, if the Government does not follow this policy, there can be an interpellation, and the interpellation may be closed by a vote of no confidence against the prime minister.

Perhaps I had better describe briefly the French political structure at the present time. The President of the Republic is elected, as in the United States, by universal suffrage, but, after that, the President nominates a Prime Minister. This arrangement is closer to the British system than to that of the United States. The Prime Minister is responsible to the Assembly, and the Assembly can, by an adverse vote, throw the Prime Minister out of office.

In this case, the President may yield to the Assembly's pressure and nominate another Prime Minister; President de Gaulle did this when he replaced Michel Debré with Georges Pompidou. Or, the President may support his Prime Minister, dissolve the Assembly, and call a new election; that is what President de Gaulle did when Pompidou was defeated. Pompidou won the election, and his party now controls the majority in the Parliament. But, if he had lost, the President would have been obliged to resign. Practically, the political institutions of the Fifth Republic are evolving toward the British system, with a president, now elected by the people, and becoming, after De Gaulle, the leader of the majority party in the Parliament. This, I think, is the structure we have at the present time. I come now to my last point, the crisis of the old political parties.

In France, under the Third and Fourth Republics, we had too many political parties; now we have none. We still have many party secretariats, many party machines, but behind the machines there is no popular support because everyone is disgusted with the old political parties. On the right, we had what was called the Independent party. They were really conservatives, but "conservative" is such a dirty word in France that nobody dares to use it, so they called themselves Independents. They were involved in the Army's revolt and refused to follow De Gaulle when he gave independence to Algeria, so, as a party, they were liquidated in the last elections. The Gaullist party, which holds most of the seats in Parliament today, is not a party; it has neither local organization nor any program. Rather, it is a chorus that sings "I like Charlie, I like Charlie" all day long. When Charlie disappears, there will be no one to sing to, and the party will dissolve.

On the other side, the so-called extreme left, there is the Communist party, which draws its strength from the unskilled workers. You have seen, from our analysis of the social revolution, that the number of unskilled workers is declining and that their outlook on life is a protest against the industrial system and a dream of going back to the preindustrial system. The Communist party is really the most conservative of all parties, protesting against any technical progress and defending, in any case, the small man, the small shopkeeper, the small farmer, the small industrialist, the small robber, the small killer, the small anything — provided it is small. It no longer makes an appeal to the people and certainly no appeal whatsoever to the young generation. The political party that could have profited from this situation is the Socialist party; in 1956, the Socialist party protested against the "criminal and stupid war" in Algeria, as the general secretary of the party Guy Mollet put it. The

Socialists won in the national elections, and the General Secretary of the Socialist party became Prime Minister. Once in power, Mollet intensified the "criminal and stupid war" in Algeria. The Socialist party lost face, and at the present time the party has no popular support.

Perhaps all this helps to explain the significance of De Gaulle's present political position. De Gaulle successfully carried through for France the process of decolonization; nobody else could have done it. Only a general can destroy an army; he smashed the revolt of the French Army, and he only could have done it. We are thankful he settled the Algerian problem. In the last few years, France has been in a state of creative anarchy in which all these new social and economic forces I have described have emerged and begun clashing with each other. De Gaulle's rule has kept law and order during a transitional period of tremendous change. Now, the transition from the old France to the new is nearly finished. The reality emerging now behind the State is a new, free contractual society that has been progressively organized and that can now express itself politically. None of the old political parties can express these new forces in French life. Next year a realignment in France's political parties may take place. In November or December of this year * we will have for the first time since 1848 an

* The reader is reminded that these lectures were delivered in 1965.

election of the President of the Republic by popular vote. De Gaulle will be elected, I think, by 55 or 60 per cent of the vote, but his opponent will draw 30 or 35 per cent, and this person will really be elected leader of the opposition by the French people. * In this election, we are not going to elect one man and defeat the other; we are going to have two elections at the same time, both of them by the French people: that of the President and of the leader of the opposition. The elected leader of the opposition then will have enough authority to create a new party, which will be a new left-wing party, as the right-wing people will vote for De Gaulle. When De Gaulle resigns, after two or three years, the man who ran against him this fall and lost, the elected leader of the opposition, will have a very good chance to become

* The Mayor of Marseille, Gaston Deferre, has just been trying to create a Democratic Socialist federation on the line of the Kennedy Democrats here in the United States, to unite the Socialist party, the Radicals (moderate left), and the MPR (Catholic party). For the time being, he has failed; all these groups are unable to agree, and Deferre has withdrawn his candidacy for the Presidency. But, everywhere there is a revolt of the rank and file against the party leaders, and it is quite possible that in October, just at the eve of the electoral campaign (which will last only one month), a committee of personalities drawn from the universities, the trade unions, the farmers organizations, and the youth movements may draw up a program, nominate a candidate (probably again Deferre), and call on all those who agree with the program to vote for the candidate. If their candidate gets enough votes (25 to 30 per cent will be enough) he will then have received from the people enough authority to launch again the idea of a Democratic Socialist federation.

our next President. These, briefly, are some of the changes that are taking place in France at the present time and that provide the basis for our inquiries in the next lecture.

II

THE NEW EUROPE

IN the first lecture we considered the sweeping transformation now taking place in France and that this
transformation is a result of a fact and two choices. The
fact and the first choice — the "baby boom" and the flexible planning policy — we have analyzed. The second
choice is my topic for this lecture, namely, the decision
to commit ourselves to the unification of Europe. France
made this choice rather quickly, due to the influence of a
private organization called the European Movement, in
which I have been active since the beginning. It
may interest you to know that within the movement,
from the very beginning, two attitudes toward the means
to be used in unifying Europe prevailed. All of us were

internationalists; no one thought of Europe as a new nationalistic state, patterned after the governments and nations of the nineteenth century. We wanted to build something new, in a new spirit, to be at the service of the world community. But we belonged to two different schools of thinking, which, in our view, are presently giving rise to the two political parties of the Europe of tomorrow. We are working together now to create Europe; when Europe has been created, we will oppose each other.

One school of thought is made up of proponents of economic liberalism, of "free traders." These people would like to have world-wide free trade, with no tariffs, no trade barriers, and an international market functioning on the principle of free choice. But, realizing that this dream was not yet attainable on the world level, they launched the experiment among the six countries of Europe: France, West Germany, Italy, Belgium, The Netherlands, and Luxembourg, who were ready to destroy tariffs amongst themselves and to create the European Common Market.

The other school, to which I belong, has visualized the creation of a world economic order, with international rules of conduct and behavior controlling economic activity, with international economic policies on the most important problems, and with world authorities to enforce these rules. But, like our opponents, since it was not yet possible to achieve this on the world level, we, too, were ready to begin among the six European countries. For us, the most urgent task in building Europe has been to coordinate economic policies, not simply to reduce tariffs and let it go at that. I may say that at the extreme limits, these two policies are contradictory. By pursuing the first policy, internal markets would disappear, ultimately, and there would be a single world market; the second policy leads at the end to one vast world-wide internal market so organized as to eliminate international trade.

Since the beginning, these two tendencies have been present within the European Movement, a majority of the Germans and Dutch being on the side of economic liberalism and a majority of the French, Italian, and Belgian members favoring some organizing of the economy. After a lot of discussion and after our attempt to create a common European military organization — the European Defense Community — failed, we negotiated and signed the Treaty of Rome in 1957 and created the European Economic Community. The treaty establishing the EEC — what you in America call the Common Market — represented a democratic compromise between the two tendencies. Article II of the Treaty of Rome states that the aim of the six countries — France, Italy, West Ger-

many, Belgium, The Netherlands, and Luxembourg —
is to realize amongst themselves a sustained balance
growth of their production and consumption through
two measures: a common market, a customs union organized over a period of years behind a European tariff wall,
whose average external duty is to be the average of the
average of the previous national tariffs; an increasing
coordination of our economic policies.

Thus, the treaty reflected a delicate balance between
the two tendencies. The fact is that during the past years
we have made progress toward the full application of
the treaty in a not very coordinated way, because our
two legs have not moved with the same rhythm. The
"right-wing leg" ran, and we are now ahead of schedule
in the reduction of internal tariffs. We have already reduced our tariffs amongst ourselves by more than 60 per
cent, the European tariff is ready, and we could without
difficulty fully realize the customs union in 1967. But,
unhappily, our left leg has lagged, because it is a little
more difficult to coordinate economic policies than it is
to reduce tariffs. In one case you deal only with trade, but
in the other case you deal with production, and this com-
pels you to face the changes of structure in the whole
of a country's economic life. In the first lecture we considered the changes that are going on in France. These
changes, however, are painful and must be guided with

tact and patience, so we have not advanced as rapidly in the coordination of economic policy. Still another reason for our slow progress is that we dealt first with agricultural policy, the policy the most difficult to coordinate. This, I believe, was the right decision. Now it is done; now that we have a common European policy on agriculture, I think that we are going to settle the other problems more quickly. Our success in establishing a common agricultural policy for the six countries in the EEC shows that miracles are possible. All the other problems will be settled because, although they may be difficult, they are less difficult than the agricultural policy.

As you may know, after two or three years of hard discussion and confrontation, we finally reached a conclusion last December (1964). We were able to reach a conclusion because of the very strong political structure that we erected in this process of European unification. We created two institutions in the Treaty of Rome: the European Economic Commission, composed of nine people who are nominated by the national governments but are independent of their governments and are really European leaders, and a council of ministers representing the six national governments. At the present time, we must still obtain a unanimous agreement among the governments in order to act. After the first of January, 1966, it will be much easier, because then the commission can make its decisions by majority vote. Practically, we succeeded in having a common agricultural policy approved by unanimous consent because the Commission of the European Economic Community made proposals; these proposals were discussed then refused by the Council of Ministers, who represent each of the six governments. Then, the commission brought forth another proposal; it too was refused by the Council of Ministers. Thus the discussions went on; at the sixth, nearly as in the Bible, the Walls of Jericho "came tumbling down." At last, a proposal of the commission was finally accepted unanimously by the Council of Ministers.

Since last December we have been putting the finishing touches — we still have a certain number of points to settle and six months' work, but the most important decisions have been taken — to a piece of European legislation that compares with the Agricultural Adjustment Act of Franklin Roosevelt in 1933. It is a very complicated and detailed piece of European agricultural legislation. If it had had to be discussed in our respective parliaments, fifty years at least would have elapsed before enactment, but we did it in two years. At the same time, without anyone taking notice we, in December, established the European price of wheat, calculating it in a European unit of account, so that already we have taken the decision in favor of the monetary unification of the six countries of Europe. It is now impossible for any one of the six countries to devaluate his currency or to re-evaluate it because to do so would change the whole setup of agricultural prices. The consequence of every national price being expressed in a European unit of account is that now we must create the structure of the Federal Reserve Board for Europe. The political decision of monetary unification, however, was taken last December.

Apart from the coordination of agricultural policy, we (and by we I mean those of us in Europe who envision a new Europe organized along supranational lines) have commenced a number of studies on other European economic problems. A coordinated policy on European transportation is ready now for discussion in the commission of the EEC, and I think it will be adopted without much difficulty.* We are still engaged in serious discussion on a European policy for using various sources of energy. This involves stating the proportions of coal, petroleum, gas, hydroelectric power, and, perhaps, atomic energy for civilian industry that we are going to use in the next ten years. For this we need to come to an agreement because the present differences in the na-

* It was adopted 15 June 1965.

tional policies are creating quite a lot of waste. We have made some progress in coordinating social policies, especially concerning minimum wages and social security.

We are just now beginning to face the problem of the coordination of investment in some sectors of the industries, chiefly in the automobile industry because this industry has been progressing much more quickly than the average industry. The automobile industry produces twice as much as the others and as much as the increase of the consuming power, so that certainly we are heading toward a crisis in this area unless some common policy is worked out among us or in the EEC. The rate of consumption does not increase fast enough to absorb all the increases of production in the automobile industry. It is necessary now to make less investment for the increase of production and more investment for the increase of productivity, for the reduction of costs, and perhaps for the creation of marginal and complementary lines of production in television sets, radio sets, and industrialized parts for the building industry, in order to be able to shift a part of the production of our automobile plants. Discussion on this problem is taking place at the present time.

Finally, three months ago, the Economic Commission in Brussels presented a five-year programmation of economic production for the six countries of the EEC. They call it *programmation* rather than *planning* because the word *plan* was used in Germany by Hitler, and our German friends abhor the word, so in European language the commission calls it *programmation.* (In French it is translated by *le plan,* and in German, as our German friends are very musical, it is translated either by *Concertation* or *Harmonization.*)

In this present situation we are compelled to face two new problems that have been brought to us from the outside. One is the problem of our relation with the industrialized countries, chiefly the United States; the other is the problem of our relation with underdeveloped countries. The first is being dealt with in the Kennedy round of negotiations at Geneva; the other has been treated at the United Nations World Conference on Trade and Development.

Now, as to the Kennedy round. You may recall the proposals of the late President Kennedy that urged world-wide negotiations among all countries, but chiefly between the United States and Europe. The idea was first to encourage Great Britain to become a member of Europe and then to eliminate all tariffs everywhere when the trade between the United States and Europe, including Great Britain, amounted to more than 90 per cent of the world trade. He also proposed general negotiation for a reduction of 50 per cent of all tariffs. Do you see how this proposal affected the movement for European economic integration? If it had been on the same line as the Treaty of Rome, that is, on the world level or on the Atlantic level to reduce tariff, and, at the same time, had sought to coordinate economic policies, it would have been all right, but the proposal was only to negotiate the reduction of tariffs. As such, it disrupted the delicate balance realized by the Treaty of Rome between the right-wing — the free traders — and the left-wing — the coordinators — parties, between those who wanted to reduce tariffs and those who wanted to organize markets. Thus, the Kennedy proposals raised a very serious question of commitment to the Treaty of Rome, whose object is to create a common market among the Six, behind a tariff whose average is the average of the former existing tariffs among the members, and nothing else. At the present time, the European tariff already has been reduced by 10 per cent from this average and is lower than both the British and the American tariffs. Since we have been building Europe through the approach of tariff reduction, but not yet through the coordination of economic policies, the Kennedy proposals have created many difficulties for us. Many of us oppose reducing external tariffs before the coordination of economic policies has progressed sufficiently to establish in Europe both a coordinated economic policy and a strong political structure.

These same difficulties appeared first at the time of the negotiation between the Six and Great Britain. Great Britain refused, you may recall, to enter the Coal and Steel Community, which was established in 1951; she also declined to take part in the European Defense Community. Her refusal was used as an argument in France to defeat the Defense Community in Parliament in 1956. When we created the European Economic Community, Great Britain opposed the EEC by forming the European Free Trade Association and failed. Finally, when Great Britain decided to request membership in the community, it appeared rather early in the negotiations that our British friends were still thinking of the EEC as a free trade zone and not as a coordinated economic community. The British conception of the EEC was reflected in the language they used, and, I might add, the language you use in the United States very often in speaking of the British entrance into the Common Market. The term *common market* is misleading; men do not enter into a market. Goods circulate in a market, but men enter into a community. I have shown you that the technique of the Common Market was one of the two techniques designed to create a European community, the other one being the coordination of the economic policies. It was the coordination of economic policies that the conservative British Government was not ready to accept at the time. It must be recognized that it was chiefly difficult for Britain to accept the European coordination of agricultural policy, because to do so would have obliged Great Britain to abandon the preferential treatment given to the Commonwealth countries and even to establish against imports from the Commonwealth a tariff that would have favored imports from Europe. The tragedy was that Great Britain, at that time, joyfully sought to marry the young European girl, but without divorcing the old Commonwealth wife. Such bigamy is rather difficult to accept. May I give an image of the situation.

After the Second World War there was a family that had lost everything. All the brothers and sisters decided to get together in order to rebuild the family house. A prodigal brother refused, however, to join the others and wandered away into his own wilderness, but when the walls of the house were standing and only the roof remained to be put on, the prodigal brother, realizing that being alone was not very good for his growth, came back and asked to enter the family house.

The whole family rejoiced and said, "The prodigal

brother has returned, let us rejoice, and in his honor let us kill the fatted calf."

"Yes," said the prodigal brother, "but one must buy the calf in Australia."

Upon hearing this, the elder brother immediately threw the prodigal out of the family house without consulting the other brothers and sisters before doing it. That move has created some tension in the family since then.

This was the situation. Perhaps things have changed a little now. With the Labor Government, which has been introducing planning into Great Britain, it will be possible to make special agreements on the coordination of transport policy, the coordination of the energy policy, and the coordination of investments in the automobile industry. For the time being, we can seriously consider the problems concerning production, but for the moment set aside questions of tariffs and trade and begin to build something with our British friends until the time when they will be able to accept membership, not in a common market, but in a real European community with supranational political institutions.

The important Kennedy round negotiations are still going on in Geneva among the delegates of the United States Government, the British Government, and of the

Commission of the EEC. Some people — and many
Americans — do not realize that in the Kennedy negotiations the Commission of the EEC, whose headquarters
are in Brussels, negotiates for the Six. This is very important; still, in these negotiations we face a number of
problems. I have no time to analyze them all. The technical ones — the problems of distortions, of the calcula-
tion of customs values, of what is called "administrative
protectionism" — I believe are in the process of being
solved at the present time.

Yet, two important problems tangle these negotiations.
One, again, is that of agricultural policy, because the
same policy does not exist in the United States as in
Europe. We have to realize that there are two types of
agriculture: the extensive agriculture that is dominant in
your country and in Canada and in Australia, as a result
of which one gets a low yield per acre and a high productivity per man at a low cost; and the intensive production methods, prevalent in Europe, by which we
return to the soil all the fertility we take out, thus yield-
ing higher productivity per acre, but a lower productivity per man at a higher cost. These two types of agriculture should not be compelled to compete with each
other, because the world, at the present time, lacks food.
One-half of the world's population is suffering from hunger, and we need, therefore, an increasing agricultural

production, both in intensive- and extensive-producing countries, even with the knowledge that not enough people will be able to buy what we are going to produce. We must, therefore, avoid competing with you on the so-called free market, because then all the prices would go down, and one-half of the world would suffer from hunger because they are too poor to buy the food they need. It now appears that the negotiations are moving toward confrontation between our different price policies for farmers. We must, in these negotiations, strive to give farmers everywhere a guaranteed minimum income, provided they increase their productivity at least 5 per cent per year, and we must so organize the markets by giving away, definitely and systematically, free of any charge, a part of our production in the campaign to fight hunger in the world. Agriculture is now an international social function that must be organized at the service of the whole world, both for the needs of those who can pay and of those who cannot pay.

Another difficulty involves industrial tariffs as between Europe and the United States. Are we going to reduce by 50 per cent our industrial tariffs? It is possible, I think, if we come to agreements on certain problems. At the present time, it is difficult for European industry to compete with American industry, because your industrial production exceeds ours by five or ten times. The largest

European concern is twenty-seventh, I think, on an American list. If we are going to compete with you, we must make — and we are making — a tremendous effort to organize European units that can certainly compete with yours. At the same time, we must maintain political control over these units, or they will establish a real monopoly system exploiting the consumer. You have the Sherman Act in the United States, but you do not apply it to exports. We have the same thing in every one of our countries, but we do not apply it to exports. We should, it appears, have an Atlantic Sherman Act, with an Atlantice Interstate Commerce Commission, using the experience you have had in the United States and that we have had in Europe in order to push the world's concentration, which is technically a necessity. At the same time we must provide for some control of the policies of these big companies, in order to prevent their dominating the markets.

Another problem about which you have certainly been reading much in the press recently concerns American investments in Europe. Permit me to explain to you the French attitude toward American investments in our country. We are very pleased that American investments take part in French industries and help to create new industries in our country. But foreign capital must go where we French want it to go and nowhere else. I give you two examples: In our Fourth Plan, we spent millions of francs to encourage French plants to establish themselves away from the congested Paris area, to settle their new industries in the underdeveloped regions of France, chiefly in Brittany and the Southwest. So, when American capital concentrates in the Southwest — HOORAY! But if American capital is invested in the Paris area, we are not so enthusiastic. We are trying to do everything we can to prevent this from happening. Similarly, we are concerned about the amount of, and purpose of, your investments in certain sectors of our economy. I have already emphasized the necessity of a European policy for coordinating the automobile industry. American investments in the automobile industry are welcome, provided they accept this European agreement and agree to obey the discipline that together we are going to elaborate.

Another matter is even more vexing, that of American capital taking over the majority of shares in existing French companies. Here, I must say, we strongly object. Recently, an American company bought a French plant in order to close it and thus eliminate a competitor. French workers thereby lost their jobs. We cannot allow this kind of manipulation. In another case, a large American firm bought a French plant in order to make a subsidiary of it, thus cutting expenses on scientific research done at the plant by having the scientific research carried on outside our country. The controlling company simply sent blueprints to France, and the French satellites had to put the blueprints into practical application. Now, we do not want to be deprived of the possibility of scientific research. Practices such as these by your business concerns have caused some hard feelings in France. We are in favor of outside capital, provided it goes where we want it to go and provided it remains a minor, not the controlling, interest in a French industry.

This leads me to a subject presently very much discussed, the decision taken by the Bank of France some weeks ago to sell some of its holdings in dollars and to buy gold. You must understand the situation exactly. First, you must remember that France holds the highest proportion of its reserve in dollars; only 72 per cent of our reserve is in gold. Other European countries hold around 80 or 85 per cent, and the Swiss have more than 90 per cent of their reserve in gold. The fact is, for many years the United States has acquired a deficit of its balance of account while building up a very large positive asset in its balance of trade. One of the elements — a very important element — of the deficit in your balance of account is created by American investments abroad, so that when we receive dollars in payment of an American debt, we, ourselves, are financing American purchase of French firms in France. The decision of the Bank of France to reduce, slowly and progressively, our holdings in dollars and change them into gold was intended to exert a pressure to slow the movement of American investment toward Europe. Curiously enough, President Johnson, by other means, is doing exactly the same thing on the American side. I wish to make this clear to you in order not to create confusion with the second problem.

The selling of American dollars for gold was a decision of the Bank of France, with, of course, the knowledge of the Minister of Finance, but not at all with the President of the Republic, who does not concern himself with these little things. After some time, however, the officials involved in this transaction decided to brief him on the problem. In the next press conference, President de Gaulle addressed himself for the first time to economic questions. He had never done this before because he was not interested. In his press conference he made a sweeping criticism of the whole system of international exchange of dollars. Almost all of us agree with this criticism. President Johnson erred some time ago when he declared officially that the gold standard bore some responsibility for the 1929 depression. He had forgotten that the gold exchange standard was introduced in 1924 and that, if the monetary system was responsible for the 1929 depression, it was not the gold standard. Rather, it

was the gold exchange standard — the one in existence
now and the one which, perhaps, by building money in
two countries at the same time and on the same reserves,
may be creating an international inflationary process that
could lead us, if we do not act in time, to the same end
as in 1929. So, we believe that we should abandon the
gold exchange standard now, but President de Gaulle,
in his press conference, spoke of going back to the classi-
cal gold standard. I must say here that the French economists, with one exception, Mr. Rueff, do not support this
view at all.

First, there is no possibility of going back to something
that never existed. What people called the gold standard
in the nineteenth century was really a very skillfully
managed sterling standard, controlled and animated by
the London banking houses. Our British friends are no
longer able to organize and animate the sterling standard
as they did in the nineteenth century. I think it would
be very dangerous to go to the gold standard because
the world's trade is increasing much more quickly than
the production of gold, and to do this now would launch
a deflationary process. It is quite clear that we need to
supplement gold as a reserve, not by national currencies,
but by an international composite unit, along the lines
proposed by Lord Keynes at the time of the Bretton
Woods Conference. His proposals were refused then but

were elaborated on last year by Professor Triffin of Yale University. We believe that it is along these lines that we may find a way of rebuilding a better international monetary situation. My conclusion on this point is that either President de Gaulle has not been well informed or that, as a very good poker player, he speaks of returning to the gold standard only to frighten everyone so that the proposal of an international monetary unit will appear as an acceptable compromise proposal. Anyway, I am sure that this is the solution toward which we are moving at the present.

Thus, we see that we cannot go on with the Kennedy round negotiations for the reduction of tariffs without discussing amongst ourselves a world agricultural policy and a reorganization of the world monetary policy, which, in turn, means a certain type of coordination of economic policy amongst ourselves. The time is finished when we can have purely tariff negotiations; tariff and trade are elements as well as instruments of a comprehensive coordination of economic policy.

If we look at the interrelated problems that were studied last spring at Geneva at the World Trade and Development Conference, we come to the same conclusions. Here we had to face the ordeal of the underdeveloped countries and to see things as they are. We in the advanced countries believe that we have helped underdeveloped countries. It is not true; we have not helped them. The Bible says that the left hand must not know what the right hand is doing, but, in the past five years, while our Christian left hand was giving, our free-enterprise right hand was taking away more than the left hand was giving. By the reduction of the prices of what they sell, these countries have lost more than they received in financial and technical help. The first thing to do is to change this situation. Here again we have the same kind of discussion as in the European Movement and as in the Kennedy round negotiations.

Some people say the most effective solution is to reduce tariffs and increase access to markets and to let these countries sell more of what they are selling now. If they are permitted to sell more at the reduced price, however, that will not help them at all. What these countries need is not to sell more of what they are selling now, when they are specializing in one or two export crops, but to diversify their production so as to sell less of what they are selling now and to begin selling other agricultural products or some industrial ones, since they are beginning to create modern industries. It appears to us — and on this point I spoke in the name of the French delegation at Geneva — that the most important problem is not access to markets but organization of markets for tropical goods and stabilization of prices. The underdeveloped countries would then know that, in the next five years, they could be certain of having a definite quantity of foreign currencies to use for their own economic development. The present instability of prices makes any economic development absolutely impossible. Moreover, if these countries start some new industries, which at the beginning are not competitive, it is of little use for them to know that, with the success of the Kennedy round, all of us will reduce our industrial tariffs. They will be unable to compete on the European market with American goods, which will oust them, or in the American markets with European products, which will drive them out. They need us to maintain some tariff amongst ourselves and to suppress these tariffs only for the imports coming from underdeveloped countries. If the United States keeps a 10 per cent tariff against European goods, and Europe does the same for American goods, and these duties are cut entirely for the underdeveloped countries, then these countries can have access of market through some preferential agreement, and not at all through the "most favored nation" clause of the old economic liberalism of the nineteenth century.

When we spoke at Geneva of the financial help for underdeveloped countries, I moved a resolution that was passed by a nearly unanimous vote. Each of our countries committed itself to devote to the help of underdeveloped countries at least 1 per cent of its national income. This resolution was passed by a quasi-unanimous vote, with the abstention of the Russians, who said that, of course, the others — the capitalists, the colonialists, the imperialists — had to grant these funds as reparations to the countries they colonized, but as the Russians never colonized anywhere, not even in Siberia, they had no obligation whatsoever. They agreed to do everything they could, but they refused to make any definite commitment. All the others accepted this definite commitment of 1 per cent. It is very little, but it is a beginning. We believe, moreover, that the best way of using the financial help to underdeveloped countries is neither through bilateral agreements, in which you have always got some form of paternalism, nor through United Nations universal organization, in which there are many delays, but by regional agreements.

With regard to aid to India, which was organized under the initiative of the World Bank but with the United States, Great Britain, Europe, and Japan taking part, these seven or eight nations negotiated with India the help they could give for the realization of the Indian Third Economic Plan. I think it is through regional negotiation between groups of nations giving aid and groups of nations receiving it and through a general discussion of these countries' development plans that we can give the most important help to these nations.

I now come to my conclusions about Europe. As you have seen, two different attitudes presently prevail concerning both European economic integration and aid to underdeveloped countries: the attitude of the old economic liberalism, expressed as *laissez faire, laissez passer*, and the reduction of tariffs; and the attitude of the planners, who insist on coordinating policies, organizing markets, and stabilizing prices. As you have seen, these attitudes confront each other in every one of the problems we have been discussing. We believe that these two attitudes will ultimately be reflected in the two political parties of the Europe of tomorrow and that we need to make a compromise between them, as we did in the Treaty of Rome. In the Kennedy round negotiations, in our discussions at the World Trade Conference to realize these two different types of outlook, we must try to respect each other's point of view and try to work together in order to establish a compromise that takes into account the position of every one of us. It is only when we are conscious of different outlooks that we can negotiate a democratic compromise. You see that all of this brings us to looking beyond the economic point of view to the necessity for getting together to frame all the important problems into a world-wide policy. The other aspects — the noneconomic ones — the military and foreign policy aspects of this problem I am going to speak on next.

III

CHANGE AND CHALLENGE

I have described the positive elements in the contemporary evolution of France and Europe. We have seen that everything in France is changing, is in a state of what I have called creative anarchy, is fermenting within the framework of law and order, presided over by General de Gaulle. We have seen that European economic unification is progressing, and progressing more quickly than had been expected at the beginning. In this final lecture we come to the problems of defense and of foreign policy. Here there is a complete disarray in both thought and institutions, because things are changing in the world as they are changing in France and in Europe. We Europeans must adjust ourselves to new conditions. On many issues, at the present time, we are advancing solutions that are not the same as those you hold to, here in the United States. Unhappily, we cannot present alternative proposals, because on these problems we, as Europeans, do not yet agree amongst ourselves. So, there is much disorder and anarchy, and there is not yet much that is creative on these problems. I am going to try to analyze some of these tangled issues, in order to show the difficulties we face, and to suggest some solutions.

Now, first of all, what are the essential elements in the international situation? Presently, there exists a balance of power in the world, between the United States and the Soviet Union. This balance of power is such that the two big countries who have the greatest responsibility in this matter consider an atomic war impossible at the present time. Instead of full-scale war, they struggle for influence over other countries in what is called peaceful competition. This confrontation between the United States and Soviet Russia assumes various forms: economic competition, financial aid, political influence, and guerrilla and civil wars inside a country. Up until now, however, each time the risk of actual war has loomed — even a conventional war — everyone has drawn back in time. We hope this restraint will continue. This balance of force in the world has permitted everyone, within the two big coalitions, to pursue their own policies with greater freedom of action. Such is the case, particularly in the East where, as a result of the conflict between the Russians and the Chinese, a great number of Communist parties have refused to take sides. At the recent meeting in Moscow of the Communist parties, many parties refused to attend, and those who did come did not agree with the Russians' proposals. There is a tendency toward polycentrism in the Communist movement, which means that we must face national communisms, each differing more widely one from the other and sometimes quarreling with each other. Thus, increasingly, opportunities for diplomacy are opening up, provided we avoid taking a position that would reunite under Soviet or Chinese leadership these national Communist regimes. Now, while the solidarity of the Eastern bloc has been disrupted, a crisis has emerged within the Atlantic Alliance. This crisis stems from the fact that, as Europe has become stronger, she wants to have a voice in the determination of the alliance's policy; yet Europe is not united enough politically to be present and to discuss with you a real European foreign and military policy.

What is the current situation in the Atlantic Alliance in the realm of defense policies? France is now creating an independent nuclear force. In my country I oppose this policy, and I may say that a majority of the French people, including the military people, do not really believe in the French nuclear force. There is a general skepticism about it; there is criticism, but this criticism is not very strong. Even the political opposition to De Gaulle is not raising the question of a national nuclear force as an important issue for discussion. The reason is that while we are building the French nuclear force we are reducing military expenditures. The reduction of expenditures on the traditional army is substantial at the present time — I do not know for how long — and larger than the new expenditures being made on the nuclear force. Too, we are reducing the length of military service. Before De Gaulle and during the Algerian War, our children went into the military service and served in the Algerian War for three years of their lives. Now, the term of service is eighteen months, and next year it will be reduced to fifteen or sixteen months. Six months ago the Government passed a law that I had been proposing in Parliament without success for fifteen years and that had always been rejected by the Socialist party when I was a member of it. This law permits conscientious objectors to perform civilian service instead of military service. Moreover, the new law provides that all students may fulfill their military service as teachers in underdeveloped countries. It is quite clear that all these changes are destroying the old French army, with its militaristic outlook, and replacing it by an army of scientists and engineers. This change is a change upon which, of course, we look with some sympathy, and this explains in part why the fight against the nuclear force is not very strong. Nevertheless, the majority of us do not believe in the effectiveness of the French nuclear force.

Two arguments for the independent *force de frappe* have been presented. One argument holds that in case of Russian aggression in Europe we cannot be certain that you Americans will take the serious risk of entering into war immediately. This view has been the result of Mr. McNamara's theory on escalation. That theory, as presented in your press, gave us in Europe the impression that if a world war began in Europe, you would be ready to wage the war first by conventional forces, then by using tactical nuclear weapons, and only at the end by your strategic nuclear power — "the end" meaning when the whole of Europe had been destroyed and the Europeans had been killed. This prospect, of course, disturbs us. The argument of the French Government is that we must have a very small nuclear force, which would act as a detonator, compelling the United States to use all its nuclear capabilities at once to defend Europe. I do not believe this argument is valid, because if you decide not to enter the war with all your force, the detonation of a French bomb would not make you do what you do not want to do. To assume otherwise shows a misunderstanding of the American mind. Indeed, I am afraid exactly the opposite would happen. Moreover, it would be impossible for you, in the case of a Russian attack on Europe, not to enter immediately with the whole of your forces, because Europe is now too strong. A Russian conventional attack on Europe and Russian occupation of industrial Europe would double immediately the war capacity of Russia. Then you would be doomed! You are, therefore, compelled, whether you like it or not, to enter into the conflict with all your forces immediately.

But recently a second argument — I would say a much more dangerous one — has been advanced, favoring the creation of an independent French nuclear force. The second argument is not that we are afraid, in case of a Russian aggression, that the United States would not enter the war; it is, on the contrary, that the United States would draw Europe into a war as a consequence of American military action away from Europe. In the present stalemate, runs this argument, there is no longer a prospect of Russian aggression in Europe. Everything on the Continent is stabilized, and nothing can move. In Southeast Asia, South America, Africa, however, things are not stabilized, and it is possible, if we are not very cautious, that the United States may get involved in a world war and drag us into war over a dispute in which we do not agree with you. In these circumstances, the existence of a European nuclear force — not just a French one — while not being enough to defend ourselves against Russian aggression, could be enough to guarantee European neutrality in a war between the United States and Russia in which we would not be ready to take part. It must be emphasized that this argument is being widely accepted at the present time; much more than the first one.

I am not convinced by this argument either. I do not believe that we can create, within ten years, a real European nuclear defense; the Russians will not let us do it. If we start, we will be handed immediately a Russian ultimatum to cease this military build-up, because the Russians fear most of all German rearmament, and the Germans would take part in a European nuclear force. The Russians prefer an Atlantic nuclear force because, after some experience, they have more confidence in the United States than they have in any other country. They believe that the United States and Russia, being the two big nuclear powers and, therefore, realizing more than any of the others the danger of a nuclear holocaust, are the two powers most likely to prevent a conventional war from escalating into a nuclear conflict. Curiously enough, the Russians would oppose less vigorously an Atlantic nuclear force, even with Germany in it, than a European one with Germany but without the United States. We must acknowledge, however, that exactly for the reasons I have advanced in answering the first argument it is not possible for Europe to be neutral in the case of a world war. Even if the war begins outside of Europe for reasons we do not like, it will be dangerous, because an aggressor would be armed to strike in Europe immediately in order to take control of the huge industrial bases of our continent. The dream of a European neutrality based on a European nuclear force is, I submit, an illusion. On both sides, the United States and Europe, we may like it or we may dislike it. The fact is that we are in the same boat, and we live or we die together. This being the case, you see how important it is, at the present time, to try to come to an agreement on the problems of foreign policy.

You should understand the crisis of the Atlantic Alliance and what we Europeans feel about it. There was a time, you may remember, when the French and British governments landed troops at the Suez Canal. Public opinion in the United States unanimously condemned this action; Russia threatened to send bombs to Egypt. The United States Government warned us that, even if Russia should send bombs it would not protect us, because the Suez expedition was a mistake. I think you were right in doing that. I, myself, had a big fight in French political life at that time because I opposed the Suez expedition. The whole Suez affair showed, however, that within the Atlantic Alliance, when you think that we blunder, you can compel us — France, England, and Europe — to change our policies, and we must yield. On the other side, when we think that you are making a mistake in foreign policy, and when we tell you about it, you ignore our opinion. This is not an alliance, it is a protectorate. You can restrain our action, but we cannot stop yours. If we want to create a real Atlantic alliance, between equal partners, we must find a way to consult together to draft a common foreign policy. We must establish machinery for permanent, continuing consultation, and, finally, we must permit both sides to veto each other's decisions. This entire problem is growing very serious now, chiefly because of the fact that we cannot support your present policy in Vietnam. It is a very delicate issue, but I shall try to explain our attitude.

We French fought to hold Indo-China as our colony. We were defeated, and we signed an agreement in Geneva that provided for a division of Vietnam into two countries for only two years; after two years had elapsed, general elections would be held in both South and North Vietnam, in order to unify the country. When the time for elections came, however, Mr. Diem refused to hold them, because he knew that he would be ousted in South Vietnam by 80 per cent of the voters. Because South Vietnam refused to hold elections, some of the people began to rebel. They created the Viet Cong movement while, at the same time, Diem destroyed the other democratic parties in the country. At the beginning, the Viet Cong was composed of the anti-Diem groups and other South Vietnamese parties. I know this, because some of my former students joined the movement at that time. Only long afterward did the insurrectional movement come under some sort of Communist control from North Vietnam. Thus, since the beginning, you Americans have been helping a South Vietnamese regime which has never been elected by any suffrage at all.

You first sent arms, ammunition, and advisers before the North Vietnamese did the same thing on their side. Finally, you "fired" Diem, but too late! You know all the difficulties that move has caused. You are trying to build up a stable government in a country where expression of public opinion is impossible. Political life is simply a continuing struggle among different generals, one taking power every month. At the present time, the war is growing more serious. The war is worsening because you are not winning in South Vietnam. You are are not winning because you are making the same blunders we

French did. You have a tremendous army — mechanized, organized — that dominates the roads but, of course, is unable to go into the jungle; the greater part of Vietnam is jungle, and your army cannot go there.

In the French-Algerian War we attempted a disastrous experiment. Some military people declared that they could not control the Algerian villages, that the insurrection spread during the night, and that the only way to protect these poor villagers, who were all pro-French, of course, was to take them out of their villages and to build fortified hamlets where they could be protected. So we moved these "pro-French" Algerians from their villages into new villages we built for them two, three, four, or five miles from the lands they farmed. They were protected, but being cut off from their land, they all went over to the rebels. Such was the harmful result of this military strategic protection of the villagers.

Curiously enough, in Vietnam, you are attempting to do exactly the same thing with your plan of creating strategic hamlets. In order to protect the villagers, you put them into new ones, and immediately they turn to the other side. Anyone who knows the mentality of any farmer would understand this, provided he was not a military man. This being the situation, you are trying to carry the war to Hanoi in retaliation, on the assumption that if the insurrection is strong in the South, it is because the Viet Cong are receiving leaders, arms, and ammunition from the North, which probably is correct now. You believe that by bombing North Vietnam you are going to compel the Government of North Vietnam to stop helping the guerrillas in the South. I must say that you cannot succeed, because the guerrillas do not obey the Government of North Vietnam and cannot be forced to do so.

I speak on this point from personal experience. I was in the French underground. When, in 1942, I joined De Gaulle, I was named Minister of the Interior, charged with coordinating from London the insurrection in France. I had to do for France what the North Vietnamese are doing in South Vietnam. From reading the last Department of State paper on the techniques of the Viet Cong, I see that they have learned quite well what we did in the French underground during the war. Quite probably, some of the present Viet Cong leaders were in our underground and took lessons in the technical organization of guerrilla warfare. As Minister of Interior in London, from where I sent money, arms, and military leaders, I was able to tell the resistance groups in France, "Do this," and I succeeded. For example, I averted an Allied bombing of the steel plants of Le Creusot, which would have killed the majority of the French workers who lived there, by ordering the resistance groups to blow up the electrical plant of Le Creusot. This was done in two weeks; work was halted for six months. I was able to tell the French maquis, "Do something," and they obeyed; but I was not able to tell them, "Do not do this." They did what they wanted to do. They obeyed positive orders, but they ignored any outside control in their own activity.

I am quite certain that the same situation exists in South Vietnam today and that the North Vietnamese Government, even if it could be convinced, is not in a position to stop the attacks by the South Vietnamese guerrillas. We must recognize this circumstance. This being the case, I am afraid you are getting involved in something that is very dangerous for all of us. If you continue to go north, and north, and more and more north — because your bombings will have no results — maybe the North Vietnamese army will go south. They have an army of 500,000 men — the one that defeated us — and I am afraid that they will not be ready at all to accept Chinese land troops arriving in North Vietnam. But the Chinese may attack South Korea, and they will take it very quickly, if you do not put ashore 500,000 of your American boys to do the land fighting. This is the direction your actions are taking you at the present time.

We in Europe believe that there is a diplomatic possi-

bility, based on the fact that all the Vietnamese hate
the Chinese — Communist or non-Communist. Ho Chi
Minh, just after the war, first directed a guerrilla action
against the Chinese occupation troops who were, at that
time, Chiang Kai-shek's soldiers. Whose soldiers they
were did not matter — they were Chinese — and he
turned against France after having gotten rid of the Chinese, not before. Then, too, the Russians have the greatest interest in stopping any Chinese advance in the
Southeast. It is not, therefore, an impossibility to build
up a Southeast Asian Federation, including the two Viet-
nams, Cambodia, Laos, perhaps Burma, and others who
would be ready to join. Such a federation would be
strong enough to protect its neutrality, which could be
guaranteed by the United States, Europe, and Russia. I
venture to say, simply, that this is a possibility. I do not
know if it will succeed, but if there is a possibility we
must try it and try it as soon as possible because the
longer we wait, the more serious and dangerous the situation will become. Again, I must emphasize that there
is a unanimous French position on this problem.* It is the

* There is also unanimous opposition to the United States' interven-
tion in the Dominican Republic for the following reasons:

(1) President Bosch was elected by a majority of a free popular
vote. When he was ousted by a military coup, you did not move. Why
are you landing troops when a popular revolt is trying to bring back
the legitimate leader of the country? Is this not a very dangerous prec-
edent for the whole of South America?

(2) In a country that badly needs an agrarian reform, you are

position of the majority of the British, who do not dare to say it officially, because they need your support in Malaysia and so cannot oppose you on your policy in South Vietnam. This is also the general attitude, from what I read in the press, in Germany, in Italy, and everywhere in Europe. Permit me to generalize a moment about this situation.

When we deal with underdeveloped countries, let us not be fooled by the name they use. The underdeveloped countries are presently passing through the fifteenth and sixteenth centuries. They must build a national state out of the tribes that are the present realities. In some newly independent nations, like the Congo, the national state does not exist. Tribes fight each other. To the Congolese tribal leaders, Mr. Tshombe is not a friend of the United States; he is pursuing the interest of East Tribe, the Tribe of Katanga. If one day Mr. Tshombe receives more help from the other side, he will move to the other side. Do not be misled into believing that Mr. Gbenye, the leader of the rebels in the Congo, is pro-Chinese. If he gets more help from the Chinese, he works with the

backing, against the poor, the big landowners, the millionaires of the high society, and the corrupt military leaders, in putting the label of *Communist* on any honest man. Are you not opening the whole of South America to Communist influence? Should Europe try, in order to save the free world, to open a third way?

(3) You are using the Organization of American States as an instrument of your own policy; is it also the way you consider the Atlantic Alliance? This we will never accept.

Chinese; if you were to offer him more help against Tshombe, he would become pro-United States the following day. These leaders are not for an independent Congo state; they are defending the interests of their tribes. In the Congo, unfortunately, you cannot build anything without Tshombe and without Gbenye; it is very difficult, I know. Maybe we cannot build any Congo state at all, at the present time, and must leave the tribes alone to fight and destroy each other. If one day the possibility of organizing a Congolese nation appears, it will have to take the form of a confederation of the tribal leaders, since the tribes are the realities.

In some other countries, chiefly in most of French-speaking Africa, matters are already a little more advanced. National states have been created there, and they are attempting social experiments. They use familiar words, but these words do not correspond to anything we recognize. Most of these states are engaged in "planning" — but planning what? Take for example the Ivory Coast. The Ivory Coast is the only French-speaking African state that is placing the whole future of the state on private capitalism and opening the country to free enterprise. Yet, the president of this state, Mr. Houphet Boigny, was a member of the French Communist party ten years ago. That is why he is so much for free enterprise! I have been in Madagascar, an island that for long was dominated by the central tribe of the Hovas, who exploited the tribes of the coast as slaves. At the present time, the Government of Madagascar is a Socialist government run by the former slaves of the coast, and the slaveowner party, the aristocracy of the Hova, naturally, are in opposition to the government of their former slaves. Being in opposition to the Socialist party, they organized a Communist party, of course. This Communistic–inclined party of Madagascar is headed by a Protestant clergyman, who is the mayor of Tananarive, and it is made up of the aristocratic former slaveowners of the country. So, let us not be deceived by the labels these people use. Rather, let us try, by international agreement, to establish a military neutralization of all the underdeveloped countries along the lines of the agreement the Big Four made for Austria after the war. Let us all agree to cease selling to, or giving to them, all the arms and ammunition that are so obsolete that we cannot use them any longer, and let them acquire their political experiences in peace, because they will change.

This is the policy we are presently pursuing, with some rewards, I must say, in Algeria. Mr. Ben Bella and the Algerian Government threw out one million Europeans formerly living in Algeria — I do not say French, since the majority were of Spanish or Italian origins — and the Ben Bella government seized all the lands of these people without paying an indemnity. Now we are giving the Algerian Government money in order to operate the land they have taken from us, and we are sending French people to help them. We have, at the present time, fifteen thousand French teachers in the Algerian schools, more than we had when Algeria was supposed to be French. We are giving Ben Bella 900 million francs every year, part of which is for loans on specific projects discussed with the Algerian Government, and the rest as a general loan, which they can use for what they want. There is much waste and many mistakes, because the Algerians are just beginning to create a modern state; it will take at least five or six more years, but we are going to help them, with the aim of building ties between Algeria and France, and we will keep the same policy with Boumedienne or with any other leader who may take power. The curious thing is that just now Algeria, Tunisia, and Morocco have been sending delegates to Brussels to ask for an association treaty with the European Economic Community. It may be that in ten years they will become full members of the European Economic Community; it is not entirely impossible. It is our opinion that we must let the underdeveloped countries do what they want politically without any interference and be always ready to help by sending food, by sending technicians, by sending teachers, no matter what their government is doing. This is the way to help them emerge from the disorder through which they have inevitably to pass at the beginning, and it is a way to avoid international conflict.

Now, before concluding, a few words on some other international problems. There is, at the present time, a crisis in the United Nations. I am not going to speak of the financial aspect of the crisis, of the fact that some countries, including France, have refused to pay for the monetary expenses incurred in the so-called peace-keeping operations decided on by the General Assembly, when the charter of the United Nations places such operation only in the hands of the Security Council. It is impossible now to persuade French public opinion that France should pay for an operation against which she voted, the aim of which appears to have been to spend a lot of money and human lives to destroy Mr. Tshombe as leader of the Katanga in order to establish him as leader of the whole Congo. Really, this is a policy that cannot be sold to French public opinion at the present time; we must therefore find another way to settle the problem.

I may say that the other way is to reorganize the United Nations. I have attended many international conferences, including the latest Conference on World Trade and Development. I must say that, when you have

122 nations represented and you must hear 122 ministe-
rial speeches, repeating and contradicting themselves,
but never carrying on real dialogue; when, after working
on committees you still must hear 122 speeches on every
problem, you get fed up with it! We avoided the catastro-
phe of a complete failure in the trade and development
conference only because at the end the president of the
conference said, "Now, I am going to make proposals,
and to help me draft these proposals I shall nominate a
special drafting committee of individuals, which will
conduct secret discussions." As it turned out, these individuals were the heads of the United States delegation,
the French, the Belgian, the British, the Indian and
African delegations, and one South American delegation.
The seven of us (including the Egyptian President), discussed freely, because we did not have the other members of our delegations looking over our shoulders. You
know that in any international conference, when the
leader of a delegation begins to negotiate, there is immediately a turmoil behind his back. Members of his
delegation start whispering, "He's capitulating; the
world is coming to an end," and they become terribly
distressed. When the heads of delegations are alone, as
individuals, without public reports to make, and with a
secretary to take notes, they can negotiate. In three days

we reached a unanimous agreement, and the governments had to accept it.

This experience with international conferences shows
that the only effective way to conduct business is to have
a small group discuss the issues and present useful proposals. I believe we should return to the competence of
the Security Council, provided two corrections are
made: First, enlarge the Security Council on a geograph-
ical basis in order to have two permanent members from
Asia, two from Africa, two from Latin America, regu-
larly, in addition to the present members; and, second,
negotiate some agreement by which the veto exercised
by the five big powers would be progressively reduced.
I do not think the veto can be eliminated now, but it
could be put under some rule, in order to be used only
in exceptional circumstances, not every time. It is the
abuse of these voting rights that has destroyed the Security Council in the past and brought decisions from
the Security Council to the General Assembly. Realistic-
ally, I do not think one can get decisions from an organization of 122 voters. The experience of the United Nations shows that if you want to be efficient you must first
strengthen the pillars of regional associations and from
these regional pillars build the world house on solid
foundations.

The German problem still troubles the world and especially European-American relations. Our German friends are pressing us to try again for German unification. We must have no illusions. In Moscow, I had a fifteen-hour discussion with Mr. Khrushchev. It is quite clear that one thing on which the Russians at the present time are adamant is any kind of German unification. If we in the West want to reunify Germany, we must try a different approach, with the help of the Eastern European governments. There is a new factor at the present time. The Rumanians, the Hungarians, and the Poles want some independence from the Russians, but not to the point of breaking the military alliance, for they will remain under Russian military protection as long as they fear that the Germans will demand restoration of the lost territories of the East. Still, they want to shake loose from the Russians, and some of these countries have already sent delegates to Paris, asking for more cultural ties, trade agreements, and even a possible treaty of association with the European Economic Community. We should explore what may be possible in this direction, because if we succeed in attracting the Eastern European countries, including Eastern Germany, and if we could sign a treaty of association with them, then our Western friends could recognize officially the Oder-Neisse line. Then it would be possible to achieve German unification with the agreement of the Poles, the Czechs, the Hungarians, and the Rumanians — and the Russians will have to accept it! The Eastern Europeans may become reconciled to the reunification of Germany if there has been progress in their relations with Western Europe and, perhaps, an association treaty signed by the EEC and Germany and the whole of the Eastern European countries, including Eastern Germany.

Now, these are some problems as we in Europe see them. We have not discussed very seriously either with you or among ourselves the German problem, partly because French policy on this question is not exactly the same as the German policy. This is why I believe it is absolutely necessary for us to create immediately a European political authority, along the same lines as the Economic Commission of Brussels, to consider questions of foreign policy. This authority should be made responsible to a European parliament elected by universal suffrage. On this point, many of us in France disagree with the French Government. General de Gaulle says that we must try to build up a common European military and foreign policy and that then we will have the basis for the creation of a European political authority. We believe, on the contrary, that if we create the European political authority, then we will have the machinery to discuss and to elaborate a common European defense and foreign policy. We have differences of outlook in Europe, but at the present time, the differences are differences between France and Germany. If both countries would join a European political authority, the differences on foreign policy would then be between one European party and another European party. These two parties would have to compromise or go to the polls; the European people would vote, and one of the parties would become the majority and the other party the minority. Then we would have a common European defense and foreign policy. I believe this step is absolutely necessary because Europe cannot discuss with you as long as it has no unity. The Atlantic Alliance is not now an alliance; it is a protectorate. You decide, and we obey. It is quite clear that little can be decided through consultation with seventeen European nations. It is impossible! Europe must speak with one voice. We are responsible for this lack of a common policy, because we are not united enough. I believe that we must unite.

You could help us unite by saying that from the day when Europe is politically unified you will maintain permanent, close consultation with the head of the European community on every problem, without any exception. You would promise that, in the case of serious international conflict, you would not use the atomic bomb without first getting the assent of the Europeans.

Statements such as these would further the unification of Europe and the beginning of a new, real, equalitarian partnership inside the Atlantic Alliance.

We really do not want — even De Gaulle, I think, does not dream of it — Europe as a third force. We may, perhaps, in our economic and social policy, with our flexible planning and our steps toward realizing industrial democracy, show other nations a third way between American capitalism and Soviet communism. This is possible — a third way, yes, but not a third force. We are, in fact, linked to you. Our fate is your fate, and your fate is our fate. We are in the same boat; we cannot avoid it, and since we are in the same boat we must make the decisions together. It is this new, real, and strengthened Atlantic Alliance, resting on an equal partnership between the United States and a United Europe, that we want and that we hope to realize.